Copyright © 2025 True XY Pty Ltd. All rights reserved.

ISBN: 978-0-646-71650-3

First Edition

www.high-t-101.com

All illustrations hand-drawn by Lang Tambun: www.langtambun.com

More anti-woke than my Bible

Jesus C.

A total waste of trees

Greata T.

As long as it's not printed in China

Donald T.

Introduction

Whilst making a coffee one morning, I realised something dystopian going on with my housemates...

Adam was frantically searching for his guava vape, and Tom had been doom-scrolling for the last 2 hours.

"When did we become so pathetic?!"

The guys snapped back, "That's rich, Carl. You're the one drinking soy milk."

Nonetheless, something strange was clearly going on. Are we tragic exceptions or part of a wider trend? It turns out that since the 1970s, men's testosterone has dropped 1% every year.

Our eyes were immediately opened to the abundance of Low Testosterone (Low-T) habits we caught ourselves doing every day. We then asked ourselves, what would our High-T ancestors have done?

High-T 101 is the culmination of these conversations. It shares our most embarrassing habits and advises how we as men can regain our former glory.

Contents (1/2)

#	Title	Topic	#	Title	Topic
1	Placard Warrior	Social protesting	26	Cinderella Story	No show socks
2	No Hard Feelings	Erectile dysfunction	27	Clothing Rotation	Choosing clothes
3	Living the High Life	Smoking cannabis	28	Freudian Nightmares	Therapists
4	CPI Cuck	Inflation worries	29	Condiment Coward	Food sauce
5	"Was That Good For You Too?"	Premature ejaculation	30	Cringing in the rain	Using umbrellas
6	Don't Sweat It	Gym towels	31	Done and Done	Ordering steak
7	Gluten Preacher	Gluten intolerance	32	Une Beer	Foreign languages
8	Un-Frozen	Being cold	33	Elephant in the room	Being obese
9	LinkedIn Lunatic	LinkedIn posters	34	Escalator needed	Using escalators
10	Turkish Delight	Baldness	35	Chef Mike	Using Microwaves
11	Call A Flake A Flake	Assertiveness	36	Fading Confidence	Getting haircut
12	Plane Stop, Brain Stop	Aeroplane etiquette	37	Flying Fuck	Reacting to insects
13	Help on Speed Dial	DIY skills	38	Gain Haters	Getting jacked
14	In T We Trust	Religion	39	He/He	Misgendering people
15	Feminutzi	Dating Feminists	40	Free Rent	Gym overtraining
16	Hit Me With Your Best Shot	Coffee dependence	41	Hanger Therapy	Angry when hungry
17	"Press 1 For A Date"	Dating strategy	42	I'm Sorry I Exist	Bumping into strangers
18	Actions Of Affirmation	Saying affirmations	43	Home Alone	Being burgled
19	Car Maze	Car parks	44	League of Losers	Playing video games
20	All the Gear, No idea	Running gear	45	Man Vs Bear	Protecting women
21	Back in my day	Old people on Facebook	46	Little Green Man	Crossing the road
22	Bin Jenga	Rubbish bins	47	Usain Burger	Running for the bus
23	Fly Thru	Drive throughs	48	Netflix And No Chill	Watching TV
24	Chat GPLowT	Chat GPT	49	Advercrisis	TV adverts
25	Diagnosis of Dumbness	Medical diagnoses	50	Motion In The Ocean	Getting Seasickness

Contents (2/2)

#	Title	Topic
51	No Pain No Gain	Non-contact sports
52	Oh So Crazy Golf	Playing mini golf
53	Nic-Head	Vaping dependence
54	Omg!	Using exclamation marks
55	Professional Sprainer	Fitness stretching
56	Omni-Insured	Buying insurance
57	Operation Kiwi	Eating fruit
58	Some Kind Of Sick Joke	Physical injuries
59	Owners Look Like Their Dogs	Choosing a dog
60	Food For No Thought	Being vegan
61	Pick A Lane	Road rage
62	Platonic Harem	Female friendships
63	Progress Protection	Wearing gym gloves
64	Rainman	Caught in the rain
65	Reverse ATM	Gambling addiction
66	Rally The Troops	Corporate language
67	Regional Director Of Nothing	Leadership roles
68	Farm to Bin	Wasting food
69	It's A Jungle Out There	Meeting women
70	Screen Time Workout	Phones in the gym
71	Sir Limp-A-Lot	Being non-commital
72	Rich In Coupons, Poor In Life	Being cheap
73	Sleep Mode: Expert	Falling asleep
74	Orange Is The New White	Using fake tan
75	Soy Boy	Drinking soy milk
76	Stop In The Name Of MJ	Buying sneakers
77	Struck Out	Bowling dates
78	King Of The Rats	Being frugal
79	Suck It Up	Using straws
80	Voluntary Embarrassment	Retirement savings
81	The Fast And The Feeble	Choosing a car
82	The Never Ending One Liner	Using cocaine
83	The Wankathon	Watching pornography
84	Tren Train	Using steroids
85	T Positive (T+)	Mosquito bites
86	Tyresome	Changing tyres
87	Undressing Your Pride	Strip clubs
88	GTA Life	Social rules
89	Warren Bluffet	Buying crypto
90	Hyper Brainflation	Reality TV
91	Social Kamikaze	Karaoke
92	Points Millionaire	Reward Cards
93	Sustainable Stupidity	ESG investing
94	Half Price Dignity	Shopping malls
95	Selfie Sabotage	Social Media
96	Splitting Atoms	Splitting the bill
97	Temperatures At Boiling Point	Car maintenance
98	Too Much Time On Your Hands	Owning watches
99	Bug Obliterator 9,000	Killing insects
100	The Selfless Gene	Having children
101	Your Own Truman Show	Society nowadays

1. Placard Warrior

Out of the 193 countries in the world, you've struck the location lottery and are living in one of the most privileged, rich, and educated countries on Earth. Something, however, just doesn't sit right, and you feel the urge to join a bunch of jobless strangers on the street, protesting against the outrage of the month.

During WWII, Irena Sendler smuggled over 2,500 children out of the Warsaw Ghetto, hidden in boxes and ambulances. But you think you're saving the world with your homemade arts and crafts placard and a slogan you almost managed to make rhyme.

Go to North Korea and launch a revolution to overthrow a real tyrannical government. Watch how your Low-T comrades begrudge that you've ended their weekly activity by creating actual social change.

2. No Hard Feelings

Recently, you require multiple open tabs of explicit pornography to maintain a half chub during your morning turkey choke. Fortunately, the Reddit doctors have the perfect solution for you - Viagra. With this silver bullet, you confidently walk into a sketchy massage parlour, put down your mother's credit card, and demand the happiest ending they have. One hour later, the poor lady has got carpal tunnel trying to get your turkey to wake up. How naive of you to think you only needed double the recommended dose.

The North African rodent, Shaw's jird, can mate 224 times in 2 hours. Today, 52% of human males experience some form of Erectile Dysfunction, largely caused by Low-T activities.

The strength of morning boners is the North Star of male health. If your Johnson can't penetrate titanium, then it's time to put down the pornography.

3. Living The High Life

Does being up for something mean the same as being down for something? Was the moon landing fake? As you and your friends discuss these topics at length, you break into a fit of laughter at the thought of Neil Armstrong faking low-gravity steps in front of a green screen. Yes, you're all stoned again.

Mark Zuckerberg built the first version of Facebook in less than an hour. You, on the other hand, thought it was worth eight hours trying to solve the riddle of whether cleaning the vacuum cleaner would make you the vacuum cleaner.

After quitting weed, you will quickly realise that:

1) Being up and down for something is the same thing

2) The moon landing was real

3) Yes, wiping the vacuum cleaner does make you a vacuum cleaner

Now get back to work.

4. CPI Cuck

After noticing a 10-cent hike in the price of almond milk and hearing your rent is going up by $15, you declare to anyone within earshot that "the cost of living is out of control!" After a few Instagram stories about late-stage capitalism, you decide to treat yourself by scrolling eBay for a new pair of vintage sneakers, because "self-care is essential in these tough times."

The average person in Burundi earns 18 USD a month, compared with the average American who makes 315 times that. Your economic luck is not something to complain about.

Instead of being a 'victim' of a 10-cent price increase, you should be earning so many pay rises that you create inflation yourself. Walk around the supermarket with pride at the magnitude of your economic effect.

5. "Was That Good For You Too?"

It's your wedding night, and after attempting (but failing) to carry your wife to the bedroom, you eagerly show her the rose petals that you littered across her bed. After 45 minutes of kissing, she starts to seductively undress and gently lowers herself onto you. An immediate eruption occurs, the power of which has not been witnessed since the tragedy of Mount Vesuvius in 79 AD. Your wife is just as upset as the inhabitants of Pompeii. You bow your head in shame.

The average life expectancy of our ancestors was 27. That means that every day of adulthood had an urgency to it, particularly the need to breed. If you were interrupted during a long coitus, then your only chance of continuing the bloodline could have disappeared.

Do not fear modern society's shaming of your rapid fertilisation. High-five your wife on a world record-breaking finish time and prepare for round two.

6. Don't Sweat It

After doom-scrolling through motivation reels all morning, you decide to wipe the dust off your gym card and head to the facility. On arrival, you see a little banner on the wall stating "No Towel, No Entry". A sense of doom arises, and you are forced to whimper back home to collect your best Spray n Wipe, face mask and towel. Finally, you are ready to begin your virtual pilates class.

Sweat itself is completely sterile. Even once the bacteria on your skin has feasted on the sweat, your gaming keyboard still houses 5 times as much.

Walk into the gym topless, tear down the banner, burn the towels, and bless every piece of equipment with your excretion of T.

7. Gluten Preacher

You're feeling a little adventurous one evening, so you try out a new Italian restaurant. You ask the waitress for the beef ragu, and luckily remember to request the quinoa alternative to fulfil your latest self-diagnosis - gluten intolerance. A while later, the waitress has finally found the definition of both gluten and quinoa, and lets you know that they are an Italian restaurant, not a hippy yoga shack based in rural Portland, Oregon.

The ancient Greeks, Romans, and Egyptians housed some of the most powerful militaries in the ancient world; surprisingly, they consumed 50-70% of their calories from gluten-based foods like bread, porridge, and beer.

Congratulations, you've just tested your T for free without needing to go to the doc, and the results are in - It's the same as your grandma's. The solution is not avoiding the gluten; it's destroying the gluten. Master the G and you master the T.

8. Un-Frozen

You're relaxing in your climate-controlled apartment, wearing the most thermally advanced clothing mankind has ever designed. As you consider walking to the shops, you're not sure if it's too cold outside. You check the weather on your phone, put your finger out the window, and ask your mum if you'll need a coat.

When Eric the Red discovered a new Arctic land in 982 AD, he felt the -30°C climate and said 'No problemo'. He subsequently named it "Greenland" as a plan to lure his more sensitive comrades to this newfound paradise.

Being unable to control the weather is already damaging enough to the male ego. Don't think, ask or talk about the temperature. Fail this and you're just reinforcing your submission to the elements.

9. LinkedIn Lunatic

Despite being told as a child that you were special and could revolutionise the world, you inevitably joined the soulless corporate rat race. But alas, there is hope; a whole group of people who regretfully did the same, and even better, an online place for you to jerk each other off - LinkedIn. Now you can proclaim with "extreme delight" that you've been promoted to Junior Officer of Beta Testing, and have hundreds of like-minded NPCs validate your lack of life ambition with auto-generated congratulatory comments.

Greek philosopher Socrates was sentenced to death for promoting an alternative way of thinking. Even on his final day, he refused offers to escape prison and chose to die for his principles.

Comment on your connections' posts, reminding them of their childhood dreams. See with pride how their job status changes from Head of Marketing to "Fighter pilot" and "Ice cream truck driver".

10. Turkish Delight

Lately, there have been a few too many windy days. Each gust of wind triggers a rush of anxiety and presents a strategic battle as you deploy all your best tactics to shield your receding hairline from the public. Despite your best efforts, some stranger has now been exposed to your unfortunate hair genetics, which leaves you with only one choice: spend $15k on a trip to Turkey to surgically redistribute your hair follicles.

To maintain a hair transplant, you are required to permanently take Finasteride, or at least until the lushness of your locks is no longer the centre of your universe. Its potential side effects include: loss of libido, inability to orgasm, and decrease in sperm volume.

Take an old rusty razor to your scalp (no cream) and remove any speck of hair follicle in sight. Your newfound aerodynamics will give you an edge over all the shaggy-haired competitors.

11. Call A Flake A Flake

Your friend doesn't turn up to your 5-a-side football game, leaving you a man short. Again. Instead of confronting him like a man, you double-text a passive-aggressive "No worries mate". You sit there stewing for the next hour, drafting an unsent essay in your Notes app about the importance of respect and loyalty.

When Richard the Lionheart didn't like the cut of Saladin's jib, he journeyed hundreds of miles to fight a bloody war, winning several battles and retaking much of the lost crusader territory.

You don't need to reclaim the Holy Land, but you do need to reclaim your dignity. Look him in the eye and tell him he's a flake. If he bails again, exile him from the realm of your football team and take his girlfriend as a war prize.

12. Plane Stop, Brain Stop

As the airplane comes to a stop, there is a tense atmosphere in the cabin. Passengers glance at each other, wondering who will be the first to unbuckle their seatbelt. A faint click from row 34 signals the start of the race, and dozens of anxious families spring to their feet, eager to secure their place in the disembarkation order, despite it already being predetermined.

Nelson Mandela patiently waited 27 years in prison for his opportunity to end Apartheid. Yet nowadays, the thought of exiting the plane 5 seconds later than your fellow passengers sends you into a state of panic.

Use the disembarkation time to stoically reflect on the thousands of scientists across history who enabled you to experience the miracle of intercontinental flight.

13. Help On Speed-Dial

Your step-children call out to you from the bathroom, complaining that the shower isn't working. You rush in, turn it on and off, and then realise you've exhausted the extent of your DIY ability. The kids look up at you, aghast that you're not able to provide for them. Defeated and embarrassed, you shuffle away and frantically call the local plumber at an exorbitant cost.

In past tribal societies, smaller groups of people meant that each man needed to add value through a broad skill set. But with the advent of the internet and travel, you've decided to outsource everything, making you weak and reliant on others.

Restore your honour by grabbing any tools you have and bashing at random parts until the problem is fixed.

14. In T We Trust

You clasp your hands together, bow your head, and contort yourself into whatever grovelling pose you think will summon divine intervention. You mutter a desperate plea for strength because the barista mispronounced your name this morning. As expected, your imaginary friend in the clouds leaves you on read.

The God that you believe in is based on the accident of geography and time. In Scandinavia, a few hundred years ago, you would have been sacrificing a goat to Wotan and Thor. At least Thor was High-T.

To deify your T-levels, you must overthrow whatever belief system outsources your problems to heaven. Voyage to Greece and climb Mount Olympus to battle Zeus. Return down to civilisation as the God of T who can giveth and taketh life depending on how horny or angry you are.

15. Feminutzi

Your mum, several teachers and an embarrassing amount of Oprah have rewired your masculine brain into that of a raging feminist. On a first date, you endlessly monologue about the evils of toxic masculinity, including mansplaining, stoicism, and heteronormativity. Your date, who recently finished her PHD in sociology, is nodding along. When the waiter brings the bill and hands it to you, you explode in rage. "How dare you make assumptions! Give her the bill and watch how happy she is to pay." The date looks at the size of the bill in bewilderment and asks you to go Dutch. "Don't you understand," you respond, "the only way to reverse the stereotype is for women to pay". She reluctantly pays, but doesn't reply to your 18 follow-up texts.

Challenge societal expectations by going above and beyond. When the waiter brings you the bill, ask him for a quote for the whole restaurant.

16. Hit Me With Your Best Shot

After snoozing your alarm for the 5th time this morning, you proceed with your self-love routine of 50 TikTok reels and 20 vape draws. With determination, you make it downstairs to your living room and find your grandmother. She tries to lecture you about the semen crusted towels clogging the laundry basket before you snap back, "Please don't talk to me, I haven't had my morning coffee yet".

For hundreds of thousands of years, Earth's most dominant apex predator required exactly 0 millilitres of espresso each morning. But today, you struggle to initiate a conversation without your artificial morning hit of cortisol to mimic a sense of danger in your pampered life.

You should be the first male alert and awake in your timezone. If you aren't, then stay awake until you are.

17. "Press 1 For A Date"

In a rare shock, the girl you like has finally texted back after 24 hours of excruciating radio silence. Initially, you think of delaying your response to make it seem like you're unavailable. However, like a toddler searching for his mother, you crave the reassurance that she is still there.

Isaac Newton was so engrossed in his scientific discoveries that he never had time for a single date, dying a childless bachelor.

Maybe don't go full Newton, but get a more intense job and take up a High-T sport. Relationships should be arranged via your PA, who will squeeze in a 15-minute coffee date between your meeting with the President of Botswana and your cliff diving competition.

18. Actions Of Affirmation

Waking up, you instantly grab your phone and open your daily words of affirmation: "I am a born leader. I am an inspiration to others. I am a dominant, amphibious athlete!" Tears stream from your eyes; you are still trying to believe what you are saying out loud.

Thomas Edison was told by his teacher that he was incapable of thinking or learning. Irrespective of what people thought, he later became one of the greatest inventors of all time.

Do your work quietly when nobody is cheering you on. The only sound you should make first thing in the morning is the grunting from 50 pushups to kick off the day strong.

19. Car Maze

Upon returning to the car park after picking up your favourite macarons, an uneasy feeling races through your body as the colour of the level looks unfamiliar. Yes, for the 2nd time this week, you forgot where you parked. With absolutely no strategy apart from aimlessly walking through all 5 levels, you bemoan the stupid building design as you eventually find your car one hour later.

In 1577, Sir Francis Drake successfully circumnavigated 56,000km across the world in a wooden sailing boat, using ancient knowledge of stars and ocean currents. Nowadays, you struggle to remember a single colour and number combination.

Level-up your navigation instincts by sniffing out your car's specific exhaust scent. And if that fails, simply press your key fob every 30 seconds until the car answers your call, probably two meters behind you.

20. All The Gear, No Idea

It's 10:00 a.m., and after a whole morning curating motivational fitness quotes, you've decided it's time to hit the pavement. You open your closet and gear up with precision: top-tier running shoes, moisture-wicking socks, high-performance compression shorts, reflective leggings, and anti-chafe balm. Strapped in like a soldier, you check your reflection and feel ready —until you realise you forgot the arm-mounted phone holster and Bluetooth earbuds. Running will have to wait.

In the 1960 Rome Olympics, Abebe Bikila, an ethiopian long distance runner won the gold medal in the marathon without wearing shoes as they didn't fit his feet properly.

Ditch the gear. Get out there barefoot and only stop running when your ancestors' voices echo with approval.

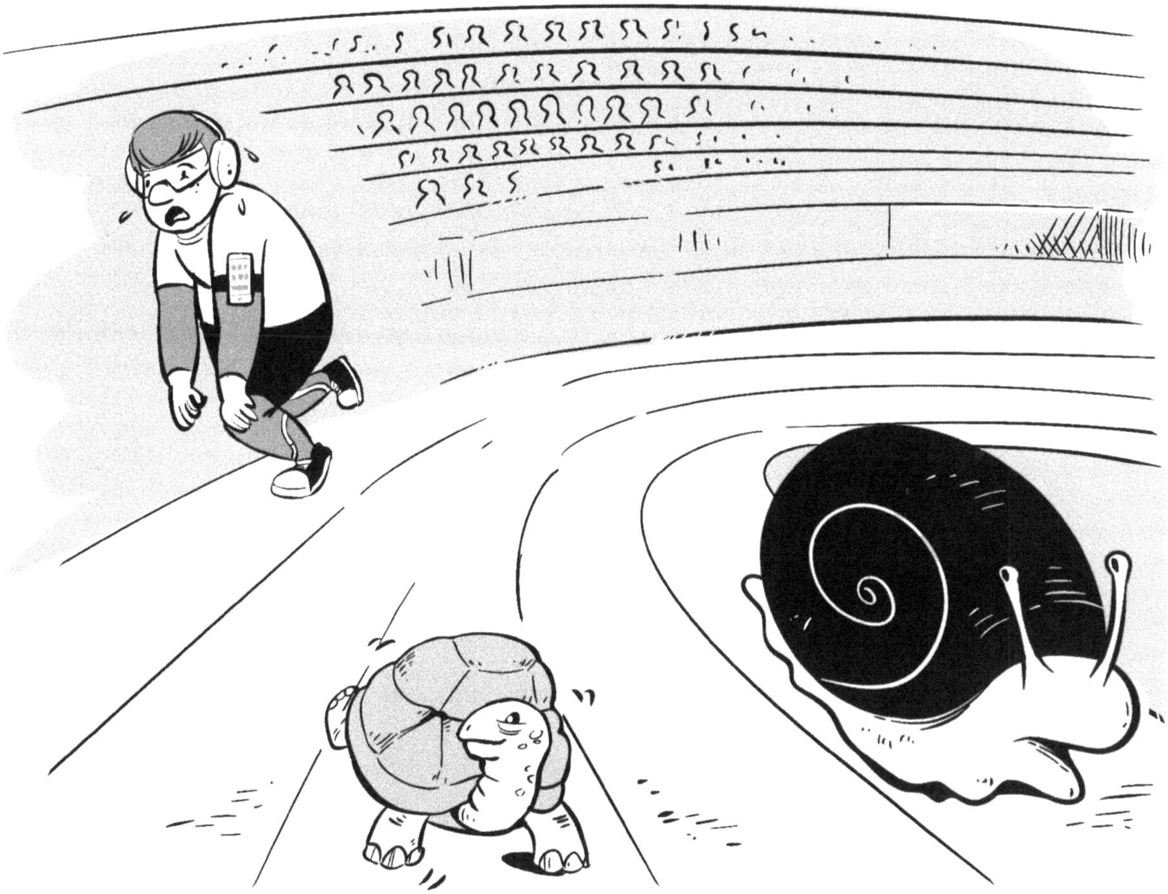

21. bAck iN mY dAy

After a long 18 years of scolding your offspring about the catastrophic effects of technology use - becoming the Hunchback of Notre Dame, brain-frying radiation, and immediate onset blindness - you decide to make a Facebook to attempt to spy on the kids. Moments later, and you're entranced in the world of reels, AI asian women, and Candy Crush Saga.

A recent article by Forbes states on average Baby Boomers are now spending over 5 hours a day on their smartphones - over 60% of the day when deducting sleep and work.

Baby Boomers, reclaim your High-T generational reputation, put the phone down, and enlist immediately. Any enemy troops will be morally stunned and be forced to respect thy elders.

22. Bin Jenga

One evening, you return home to your grotty flat-share of single stoners. As usual, the guys have decided to engage in an unspoken game of bin-jenga. The garbage piles up and each flatmate hopes the other's nerve will crack first and take it out, because the smell, weight, and 20m walk are just too much to handle.

When Eddie Morra in the film Limitless takes a super-productivity pill, the first thing he does is clean his apartment. If you've been defeated by a bin bag, you might as well just crawl back into bed now.

Immediately throw out all the rubbish in the house, which includes your Low-T housemates.

23. Fly Thru

It's dinner time, and your cravings for greasy fast food are at an all-time average, so of course, you jump off the couch, head to your car and rush to the nearest Burger King. Upon arriving, you are met with a queue of 30 cars at the drive-thru, next to an empty parking lot. Your stomach grumbles at the thought of waiting 40 minutes, but you're left with no choice; the alternative is to walk 20 meters. Plus, you can't be seen in your lazy clothes. Who knows which romantic prospects could be lurking around?

The Arctic Tern bird travels 90,000 kilometres from its breeding grounds to its feeding grounds, yet you can't walk a few meters to collect meat that another man bred, farmed, slaughtered, transported, cooked, seasoned, and packaged for you.

This is a war on T. Deploy spike strips across every drive-thru in a 90,000 kilometre radius. This will force a mass starvation of every fatty on wheels.

24. Chat GPLowT

You sit in the dark, illuminated only by the glow of your screen. "ChatGPT, how do I talk to women?" "ChatGPT, should I start lifting?" "ChatGPT, am I handsome?" You treat AI like a modern-day father figure and go to bed smug, ignoring the fact that you've just been gaslit by an algorithm trained on Reddit.

Socrates never had a chatbot to spoon-feed him answers. Instead, he roamed the streets of Athens, questioning everything and everyone until they either gained wisdom or wanted to strangle him.

Technology should serve you, not parent you. The next time you're about to ask ChatGPT how to be a man, close the laptop, step outside, and do something that doesn't require a Wi-Fi connection—like building a fire, fixing a car, or lifting something heavier than your phone.

Written with ChatGPT

25. Diagnosis Of Dumbness

Over the last few months, you've noticed a mild soreness in your arm, and after lots of worrying, symptom Googling and expensive visits to specialists, you've finally been diagnosed with a harmless genetic condition. The doctor advises you to "take it a bit lighter at the gym", as if you could.

Lionel Messi was diagnosed with Growth Hormone Deficiency and went on to score 850 goals, making him one of the greatest football players of all time.

Don't let labels and pathetic requests for empathy limit your potential. Reverse diagnose your Doctor with "Incurable lameness" and go straight for a deadlift personal best.

26. Cinderella Story

You're at a beach bar getting frisky with a curvaceous Latin woman, and she's giving you all the right signals. The next thing you know, you're heading to the beach for some steamy skinny dipping. As you get to the sand, you both hastily undress. First the shoes, then the trousers, and then the shirt. Silence fills the air, and she's got her hand over her mouth in shock whilst pointing down. You look down and see your feet in no-show socks. The deafening sound of drying genitalia echoes around you... You look back, and the curvy Latina is nowhere to be seen.

In 2002, The Wall Street Journal published an article called "A New Trend Is Afoot" about no-show socks "that hug the foot like ballet slippers". These were made popular by Lindsay Lohan, Lauren Conrad, and Jessica Simpson.

Take the ballet flats off and embrace the High-T pheromone cocktail of bare sweaty feet, toe jam, and mouldy sneakers.

27. Clothing Rotation

After a couple of weeks, you look at your walk-in wardrobe and it dawns on you that your top 10 'fits' have already been worn. This means one of two things. You can risk going out in the same outfit you wore 13 days ago, or wear a slightly less fashionable outfit and risk social exclusion. The choice is obvious to you – it's time to hit the shops and buy some new 'drip'.

For generations, our High-T forefathers echoed, "It's not about the suit, it's about the man in the suit." The key is to focus on building virtue and character, not the quality of hand-sheared merino wool in your trousers.

Now cut the drip and hit the streets in the best suit you have, your birthday suit.

28. Freudian Nightmares

Poor life habits have left you feeling down, so you decide to see a therapist. The overweight psychologist starts by pandering to your sedentary lifestyle by lying you down on a comfortable sofa. She then asks you about your traumas and 1st world problems. No matter what you say, her solutions always seem to involve additional sessions where she validates your triggers for $250 a pop.

None of the greatest men who ever lived had a therapist. Caesar didn't spend time processing trauma with Dr Jane Smith before crossing the Rubicon and conquering Rome.

Get off the sofa and use that spare cash to build a business that forces people to exercise more. This will put all the therapists out of business, and as your profits increase, so will your serotonin.

29. Condiment Coward

Your mum makes you a hearty meal of medium rare steak with mashed potatoes. But you look gloomily at it, worried it won't have enough taste. Before you know it, you've smothered it in aioli, ketchup, and three kinds of relish.

Lions don't pause mid-hunt to sprinkle Himalayan pink salt on a gazelle. They just tear in with their canines: no sauces, no side salads, and no Yelp reviews.

Food is not made for taste, it is simply fuel to hit your goals. Refusing to eat unseasoned meat is disrespectful to the lifeform that died for your benefit. See the food, eat the food, thank the mum and get back to work.

30. Cringing In The Rain

It's a rainy and blustery winter's day. Fortunately, you remembered to bring your umbrella. Whilst walking down the street, a gust of wind hits you and after a few seconds of fighting to keep control, the umbrella inverts and everybody in the street rightly looks over and sniggers.

In the Victorian martial art Bartitsu, umbrellas were used for self-defence. They held it like a sword and used the shaft for jabs and blocks, and the handle to hook limbs.

Treat your umbrella like a weapon to fight the natural elements and establish yourself as a modern-day Aeolus, god of wind.

31. Done And Done

Imagine it. You've finally got a girl to join you on a dinner date. After months of planning, the day is finally here, and for once, they didn't cancel. The waiter takes your order and you ask for the Sirloin steak, "Well done, please - The blood makes me queasy". Congratulations, you've just entered the friend zone at world record speed.

Cooking meat well done destroys heat-sensitive vitamins (B1, B6, and Folate), increases carcinogens, and reduces respect from both males and females in your community.

Don't even look at the menu, just pick out the largest piece of raw meat you can see and start the process of reverse evolution.

32. Une Beer

You find yourself in a non-English speaking country, armed with nothing but your primary school French and Google Translate. You notice everyone around you communicating effortlessly, while you fumble with your phone like a toddler with a Rubik's cube. You approach a local pedestrian, point at your stomach, and mutter "croissant?" in a tone that makes it sound more like a question for a therapy session than an actual request.

Sir John Bowring, the 4th Governor of Hong Kong, understood 200 languages and spoke 100, while you can't remember how to say your name in a country you paid to visit.

Bowring didn't learn languages to order pastries; he did it to dominate the room. Do the same, one croissant at a time.

33. Elephant In The Room

You are fat. And what's worse, you know it and try to own it. You make fat jokes about yourself in front of others to disguise your shame, such as referring to your seven deadly chins and that you are the reason they invented the double door. You can't lose weight because of a million excuses; you are too busy, you have a slow metabolism, low energy, blah blah blah.

Fat cells contain enzymes that convert T into Oestrogen, so obesity reduces the amount of T that can be carried in the blood. Knock knock, who's there? Diabetes. Diabetes who? Diabetes, you've lost your leg as well as your T. Not funny? Good, because it's not a joke.

Move more, eat less. Except protein…always eat more protein.

34. Escalator Needed

Every now and then, you need to make it to the office to show your company that you do, in fact, exist. Each time you are given the option to battle up the stairs (two at a time) or twiddle your thumbs as you ascend the slow-motion escalator of loserness. Of course, you choose the escalator every single time.

Escalators are for the disabled, elderly, and pregnant. The parties that can barely make it out of bed, let alone up a staircase.

If you're going to step foot on an escalator, do it the opposite way, and shove every able-bodied person off the side. You will be the great cleanser of escalators, protecting us from the Low-T gates of hell.

35. Chef Mike

Dinner time has come, and despite having a better choice of fresh food than any king throughout history, you grab a frozen bolognese ready meal, following the instructions to add salt and pepper so you feel like a chef. Hypnotised by your own laziness, you stare through the microwave door as you watch your 'food' go around in circles for the allotted 3 minutes.

While the average person used to spend 5 hours a day preparing food in the 1800s, we now spend only 37 minutes. Cooking, a beautiful labour of love, has been relegated to a nasty household chore, as our appetite for irradiated astronaut food has skyrocketed.

Collect all the wood and meat you can find, and send a towering column of smoke as a beacon of hope for the rest of society.

36. Fading Confidence

You notice your haircut isn't as fresh anymore, so you go to your local salon, where you sit in a plush leather recliner, discuss your hair ambitions with the hairdresser and explain that you want it to look nice for your ex's birthday party. They bring you a cup of tea and use a hot towel to soften your skin. Once the trim is done, you stride out a new man, your confidence totally dependent on the freshness of your fade.

Albert Einstein was notorious for his unkempt hair, saying that "People judge me by my ideas, not by my appearance". But as you don't have much else to offer the world, taking a compliment for someone else's workmanship will have to do.

The only ambition you should be discussing is one of the mathematical type, $T = 0 \; C(uts) \; Squared$

37. Flying Fuck

You are calmly chatting with a friend when suddenly a 6mm fly lands on your chest. As if possessed by a demon, you start flailing your hands around, shouting that you hate flies. Needless to say, you miss over and over again. Your hands slap your chest and legs as the harmless insect nimbly jumps around your body.

In the film Wanted, Mr. Sloan shoots the wings off a fly mid-air. Po from Kung Fu Panda can snatch a flying dumpling clean out of the sky with chopsticks. A fly's brain is the size of a poppy seed. If you're being outsmarted by that, then you have some serious problems.

Either practice stoic self-control and ignore the fly, or kill it with your first swipe.

38. Gain Haters

You decide that enough is enough and it's time to turn your life around. You start by lifting weights - a proven way to release stress, improve physical health and increase self-confidence. After proudly striding home from your first gym session, you are hit with a raft of concerned jibes from your mum, sister and girlfriend. "What's the point?", "I read an article that protein shakes are bad for you!", and "Girls don't like too much muscle". You think they must have your best interests at heart, so you email the gym to cancel your membership.

Spartan boys were separated from their families at age 7 and put through gruelling military training so they could defend their tribe in adulthood. But nowadays, your dedication is scorned, the equivalent of a charity rejecting your donation.

Leave the house for three months, and when returning, see how many jars of jam still haven't been opened, thus making you the hero of the house.

39. He/He

You've misgendered your workmate again. He might look like a man, act like a man, and smell like a man, but John, renamed to Jenny, is clearly a They/Them. You wearily trudge into the HR office and apologise to an overpaid and overweight pink-haired gender studies grad for your 'bigoted' behaviour.

The psychiatrist Jordan Peterson tells us to "never apologise if you have done nothing wrong". If you have to make an exception to this rule, let it not be to the middle-aged infant-minded HR manager.

Start identifying as someone who believes in only two sexes and report any Xe/Xhem for not respecting your viewpoint.

40. Free Rent

You recently started going to the gym and have already consumed more fitness content than both Ronnie Coleman and Arnold Schwarzenegger combined. But after looking in the mirror and still seeing a total dweeb, you look to a friend, Chat GPT, for advice. It responds to your worries and suggests that "you may see results if you train more regularly than once a week." You scold the AI. Does this idiot really not know about overtraining?

Michael Phelps was a big 'over-trainer'. He swam 6 hours every day for his entire career and somehow managed to amass the most Olympic gold medals in history.

Hoist your mattress into the gym and don't leave until your deltoids are too wide to fit through the double door frame.

41. Hanger Therapy

Despite having no place to be or any other time pressure for that matter, you start getting impatient with your waiter at the restaurant, "Oi, it's been 15 minutes, where is my creamy Tofu?"

A Scottish lad, Anqus Barbieri, fasted for 392 consecutive days and lost 276 pounds whilst consuming only water, multivitamins, and coffee. Yet somehow you are struggling to fast for a two hour period in between dinner and your last snack.

Every time you feel hunger interfering with your emotions, use it as an opportunity to practice self-control. If your meal is late then rejoice. If it arrives early, tell the waiter to send it back.

42. I'm Sorry I Exist

Walking down a busy pavement, you softly brush shoulders with another person. Instinctively, you feel the need to deeply apologise for such an outrageous act. They barely even hear your whimper of an apology, don't acknowledge you, and simply carry on with their day.

In WWII, retreating Russian armies flattened uninhabited villages to stop the Germans from gaining valuable wartime resources. Your almost physical contact with another person is hardly cause for panic.

If the other person is High-T, a simple "Sir" is an acceptable way to show your respect. If they are Low-T, carefully lift them up and place them out of the way.

43. Home Alone

You jolt awake to the noise of a window smashing, and hear footsteps slowly climbing up your staircase. In a state of panic, you crawl into the bathroom and lock the door, hoping the intruder will steal all your belongings and leave without a fight. You frantically call the Police, but nervously wait on hold as they're busy arresting people for offensive social media posts.

17th-century English Jurist Sir Edward Coke declared, "A man's house is his castle", which later developed into the modern-day "Castle Doctrine". It gives legal protection to homeowners to use deadly force against invaders. So what are you waiting for?

Grab the nearest weapon and storm out with your loudest war cry. The intruder will have no option but to respectfully apologise for disturbing your sleep.

44. League Of Losers

Sat down (as per usual), gaming controller in hand, you play for eight hours straight. In the real world, you are scared of small talk with your boss and paranoid about your friend chatting to the girl you like. In the virtual world, however, you defeat the Viet Cong with an M16, manage complex economies and lead entire civilisations to glory - all while wearing the same boxers you slept in. Impressive. Disgusting. Both.

Throughout the Blitz bombing campaign of London carried out by the Nazis, Churchill didn't leave London or hide in a bunker, but instead stood on the rooftops showing solidarity with his fellow citizens.

Testosterone increases when you take actual risks, not the 'threat' of losing to some infantile-looking AI bot. Delete the avatar, become the man.

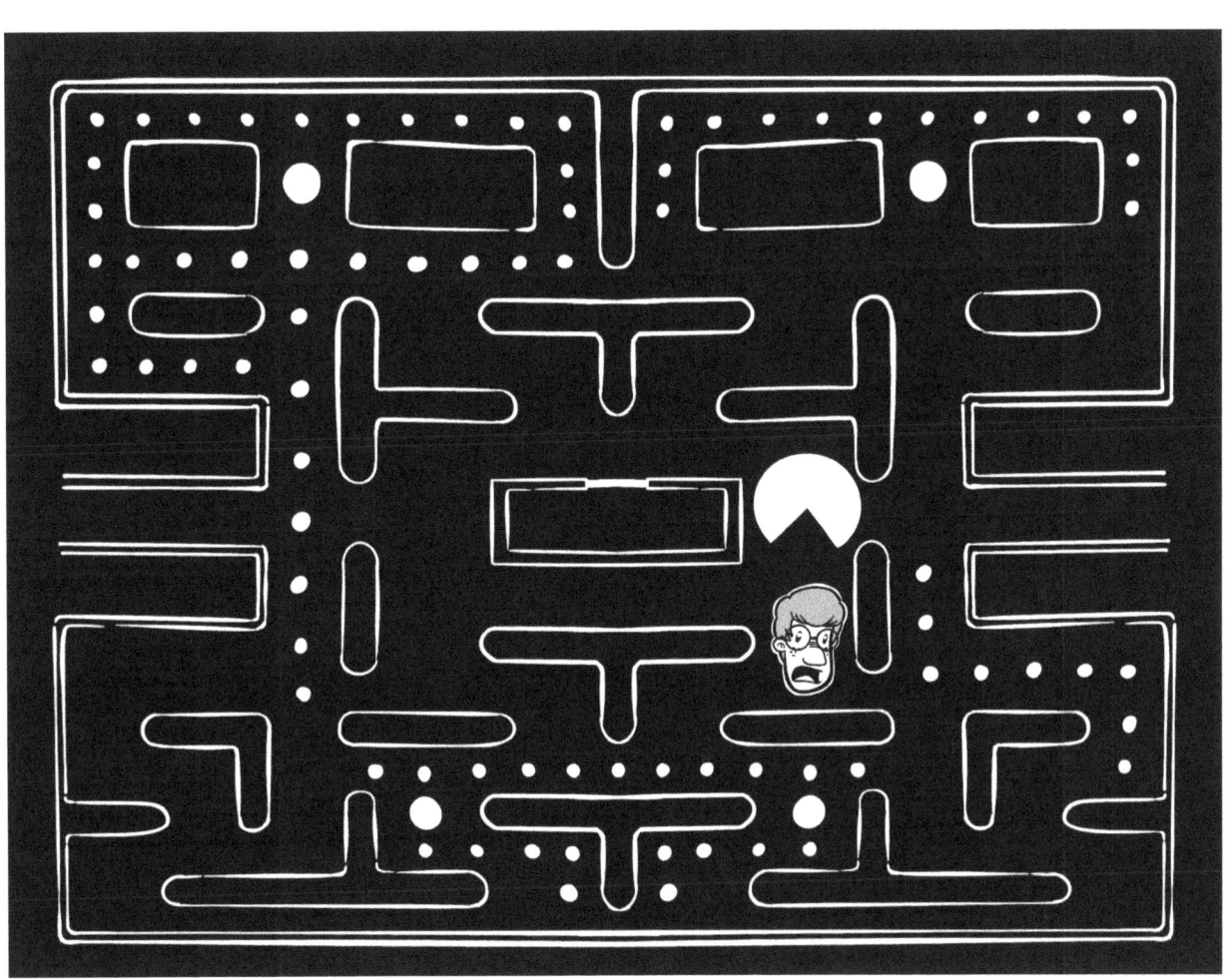

45. Man Vs Bear

You're in a nightclub with your friend Amy, and as you jiggle your hips to another Ariana Grande banger, a dodgy-looking guy walks past and grabs Amy's bum. Disgusted, she turns around and looks at you to fix the situation. Your heart races as you panic about what to do, deciding to whimper "Let's just leave it" before you report the incident to a nonchalant barman and write a 1 star review on Google Maps.

At age 9, Khabib Nurmagomedov wrestled with Russian bears and then dominated in the UFC as an adult, all while gaining a reputation as one of the most respectable fighters to have graced the octagon.

Don't outsource justice. Pop home, grab your bear costume, and maul the pervert to protect Amy's honour.

46. Little Green Man

You are on your way to see your local pot dealer, but as you try to cross the road, the pedestrian red man starts flashing. You look at the floor for instructions, look left, right, and left again. There isn't a car in sight, and a macho man naturally crosses the road. Your girlfriend follows him. Despite feeling frustrated, you wait and wait until the green man eventually lights up.

In 1963, JFK didn't wait for the green light from Congress to launch a naval blockade to prevent more missiles arriving in Cuba. His action resulted in negotiations with the Russians that de-escalated the risk of nuclear war, thus saving the world.

Take a deep breath and walk across the open road. If your T levels are running high, any oncoming traffic will wait anyway.

47. Usain Burger

You took too long to finish reading your words of affirmation and found yourself late for a job interview as a hamburger mascot. Despite your motion sickness, public transport is your only available method of travel. You see the bus arriving earlier than usual. Do you run for it?

In 1903, the Wright brothers wanted to travel too. Unlike you, though, they didn't wait for a ride; they built their ride: an aeroplane that now dominates the world.

Never run for a bus. Instead, run past the bus and all the way to the interview.

48. Netflix And No Chill

You did it! You achieved the herculean task all Low-T individuals dream of - completing Netflix. Every day, you spend countless hours sitting in front of the idiot box, staring at the achievements of others. As king of your depressing castle, you have every home comfort possible to defend against muscle usage: a footstool, a leaning headrest, and a side table for your saturated snacks.

To join the American Marines, you must complete a 54-hour endurance test called "The Crucible". This involves marching 45 miles while sleep deprived, carrying a 20kg backpack. It is amazing to think what the human body is capable of doing, or not doing, in your case.

Destroy your sofa and all accompanying devices. If your girlfriend still forces you to do a movie night, then stand in front of the TV, squatting the whole way through. She will be transfixed on your ever-growing glutes and away from the TV.

49. Advercrisis

After a gruelling day of discussing the weather, weekend plans, and last night's dream with your colleagues, it's time to head home and watch the newest episode of Married at First Sight. The couple is about to have their first kiss, your on the edge of your sofa and – bang – a McDonald's ad flashes on the screen. Disgruntled, you look over to your missus and curse, "That's the fourth bloody one so far!"

In the US, advertisements generate over $70 billion in revenue for the television industry. If they didn't exist, none of your meaningless shows would ever have been made.

Next time you want to unwind, go to the cinema solely to watch the first 15 minutes of advertisements, then leave abruptly after.

50. Motion In The Ocean

You've finally decided to embark on a 'worldly adventure', which by your standards is going on an all-inclusive cruise. As the ship sets sail, you're suddenly crippled by dizziness and nausea. You frantically rummage through your suitcase and breathe a sigh of relief when you find the seasickness medication your mum packed for you.

Ross Edgley swam 2,900km around the entire United Kingdom in 157 days. But you sit on a 15-deck, 100,000-tonne mass of metal and complain you can still tell you're at sea.

It's already embarrassing that you need a boat to travel across oceans. But if you must, pick the most feeble vessel you can find, and Poseidon will decide if you deserve to arrive in one piece.

51. No Pain No Gain

Feeling starved of male company, you enter friend acquisition mode and sign up for a local rugby team. However, when you turn up for the first session, everyone's talking about their phantom injuries and the humidity level. You feel something isn't quite right, and it all makes sense once the referee explains that this is the non-contact league.

Priscus and Verus were two skilled gladiators who fiercely fought each other in the Roman Colosseum. After a long, evenly matched battle, they both laid down their weapons out of mutual respect and friendship. Moved by their courage and honour, they were both granted freedom, a rare and powerful gesture.

Body slam the first opponent you see, drag them to the physio, buy them a beer, and watch as your brotherhood flourishes.

52. Oh So Crazy Golf

After wasting another precious day of life at your mundane office job, you're in the mood for a giggle with your work acquaintances. You attend the monthly bonding event - crazy golf. Finally, after being rejected from school sports teams due to your fear of competition, you can now compete in a chastised version of one of the most technically difficult sports.

Tiger Woods won the 2008 US Open after playing for 5 days with a broken leg and torn ACL. But some cute miniature buildings, neon lights and trashy pop music make you feel like you're living on the edge.

Acquire the largest driver you can and demolish the building. Now your Low-T colleagues can also have an authentic escape room experience.

53. Nic-Head

After nursing a beer in the park for over 2 hours, you notice an acquaintance puffing a cherry and guava vape. The sweet smell sends you into a state of craving, and the pre-vape jitters overwhelm you. As you pluck up the courage to beg him for a quick draw, he looks at you with pity and hands it over. You inhale deeply, knowing this might be the last hit you'll get for several hours.

In WWI, soldiers were given four cigarettes a day to calm their minds from the horrific conditions of trench warfare. You don't deserve to relax when the most stress you face is ensuring your work PowerPoint slides look pretty.

Put the vapers in a life-or-death situation and watch how the survivors thank you for letting them earn their smoking relaxation.

54. Omg!!!

Your mate just texted that he's not able to join you for a drink at the pub tonight. While replying, you're worried about coming across too direct, so you add a few exclamation marks to make your response seem nice and friendly: "All good! We'll find another time!!!"

Before the Naval battle of Trafalgar in 1805, Admiral Horatio Nelson rallied his Sailors by writing a sign that "England expects that every man will do his duty." But without the expected triple exclamation mark, you now interpret a simple and direct response as offensive.

It's only a suggestion though! Don't worry!

55. Professional Sprainer

You've mustered up the courage to join your company's corporate netball squad, and this week you finally get a chance to come off the bench. 5 minutes later, you're limping like you've just been bent over by a silverback gorilla. You rush to the local GP and beg to be massaged and stretched by some skinny-fat middle aged man, who insists that you need to spend the next 10 weeks humping the air and touching your toes.

Have you ever seen a Cheetah stretch before sprinting down a gazelle and tearing its head from its torso?

If you feel an ache, congratulations. You've officially levelled up from Corporate Drone to Slightly Endangered Mammal.

56. Omni-Insured

Your mate is spouting off again about his life and income insurance, convinced it's the smartest financial move he's ever made. Inspired, you wonder if you should also protect yourself against every possible outcome. After clicking through options, you're now signed up for five policies, covering everything from parcel damage to asteroid impact.

The insurance market covers over $6.8 trillion off the back of your Low-T paranoia. Whatever insurance you buy, they have done the math, and it's not in your favour.

The only protection you need is your own two hands; if an asteroid does hit, simply pick it up and throw it back.

57. Operation Kiwi

After reading in your mum's yoga mag that Kiwi fruits are the latest superfood, you pick one up on the way home. As you get ready to indulge, the fruit's natural furry texture instantly repulses your Low-T instincts, so you waddle over to the kitchen drawer to select your favourite knife and little teaspoon. You carefully slice the fruit open and begin scooping the tasty insides.

50% of humans in the Western world are nutrient deficient. 30% of a fruit's nutrients are stored in its skin, and still society deskins its apples, peels its potatoes, and scoops its kiwis.

Journey to the deserts of Mexico and put your texture tolerance to a real test by gnawing your way through a forest of jumping cholla cacti.

58. Some Kind Of Sick Joke

After cutting your finger whilst trying to slice a kiwi, you feel lightheaded and ask your mum to take you to the emergency unit. You're understandably the lowest priority, so you sit in the waiting area for 4 hours and post a dramatic selfie on Facebook in the hope of receiving an outpouring of concern. Alas, nobody comments. The WiFi must be weak here...

In the true film 127 Hours, Aron Ralston was trapped under a boulder and had no choice but to slowly amputate his own arm with a blunt penknife. His screams that echoed across the desert were a pure release of pain, not some half-baked whine for the attention you missed as a child.

Let the cut bleed out (no band-aid), delete the selfie, and devour the little kiwi whole.

59. Owners Look Like Their Dogs

You love your Cockapoo, Fluffy. He is the best friend you could ever have. When you come home from work, he jumps up to greet you, wagging his tail with happiness. It's been a difficult day of being left on delivered, so when he climbs into bed and licks your face goodnight, it keeps your loneliness at bay.

Roman legions bred Albanian war dogs to run with them into battle against Barbarian tribes. They would tear at the enemy's arms and throats, salivating as they ripped the organs from the lifeless bodies.

Rename Fluffy to Bruce, swap the pink leash for a metal collar, and release him into the wild to destroy your enemies.

60. Food For No Thought

Your arms grow thin, as does your list of friends. The cause for both is your newfound veganism. Like every new believer, trying to convert others has boundless energy but minimal logic. Even Bruce, your once-proud carnivorous dog, now shares your kale-based suffering. The two of you resemble background extras from The Walking Dead.

Humans used to thrive on eating meat and fruits alone. Does our omnivorous digestive system, developed over millions of years, not mean anything?

If you're truly dedicated to nature, then act like an apex predator rather than a nadir prey. Stalk your meal, kill with your bare hands, and feast on its heart while howling at the moon. Or, at the very least, stop pretending your quinoa bowl makes you superior to those who built the world.

61. Pick A Lane

For some reason, every time you climb into your 2003 Toyota shitbox, you feel an unfamiliar sense of urgency and aggression. You cut through traffic hurling all sorts of creative slurs at people who can neither hear nor see you - all in a desperate attempt to be the first to arrive at the next red light. The benefits are incredible - license suspension, occasional rear-ending, and a time savings of 5 minutes per year.

Philosopher Ralph Emerson coined the famous phrase - "It's not the destination, it's the journey".

Next time you feel that obnoxious rage, throw the car in neutral, jump out, and push it all the way to your destination. Watch as observers convert their rage to pure joy as they bear witness to such a feat of raw strength and power.

62. Platonic Harem

You proudly declare that you "just get along better with women", yet your main contribution to these friendships is liking their thirst traps and spilling the goss on your friends' dates. You convince yourself that having a circle of female besties somehow makes you more emotionally enlightened.

In the world of cuttlefish, the alpha male prevents any betas from getting near the ladies. So the cunning beta fish changes his skin colour and posture to resemble a female. The Low T fish then sneaks under the alpha's tentacles and starts humping all the women.

If you can't out-alpha the competing males around the girl you like, then at least convert that female friendship into a female bonership.

63. Progress Protection

After finally realising that your lack of female attention is due to your physique resembling a coat hanger, you pluck up the 'courage' to join your local gym. You make sure it's near your house, cheap, and on a 1-month trial - because God forbid you commit to a healthy long-term habit. You put on your gym gloves to prevent your keyboard-tapping hands from getting calluses (your skin's natural armour).

In 2016, English Powerlifter Eddie Hall broke the world record with a 500kg deadlift, causing him to go temporarily blind with blood pouring out of his eyes, nose, and mouth. All without a glove in sight.

Bench that minuscule weight until you've shredded all memory of sensitive skin until they call an ambulance for your lack of skin.

64. Rainman

After ten minutes jogging on a low-speed treadmill, you are sweating profusely and decide to go home for a shower. However, disaster strikes. You look outside and see it's raining, but your car is parked fifteen meters away and you don't have an umbrella or raincoat. After waiting an hour in reception for the rain to die down, you hobble to your car like a disabled chimp. But skin is waterproof. You already know that because you're going home for a shower.

In Ancient Rome, wealthy citizens would have slaves carry large parasols called umbraculum to shield themselves from the sun. If it rained however, umbrellas were not considered masculine so they would pack them away and get drenched.

Whilst the rain is at its thickest, channel the spirit of a classical legionary and charge toward your Toyota with strength and honour. Do all this whilst naked, lathered up in shower gel and claim your celestial wash.

65. Reverse ATM

Of course, you've heard "the house always wins". But the slot machine's flashing lights and jangly music put you in a trance-like state as you lose your daily paycheck in a couple of minutes. You develop a unique button-tapping strategy, despite the game being a pre-determined scam. Eventually, you trudge home to tell the kids they'll have to go hungry again. I guess you missed the chapter on "Protect & Provide".

Terry Watanabe 'won' the record of losing $204m in a single year in Las Vegas. He later had the cheek to set up a GoFundMe page for the $100k he needed for an operation.

Don't be a Mr. Terry. Set up a GoFundMe for a local Fight Club and go full Tyler Durden on the casinos.

66. Rally The Troops

Your Manager, who has a dad-bod despite being childless, attempts to motivate your corporate colleagues with various war-like phrases: "I've been battling customers all day", "We are launching a guerrilla marketing strategy", "Gather the troops into the war room.", "Let's create a battle plan", "Dave and I used to be in the trenches with this client", "The presentation is tomorrow. D-day".

During the terrorist attack of 9/11, Rick Rescorla, an employee at Morgan Stanley, evacuated over 2,700 employees despite official orders telling him to wait where he was. Even though he was an ex-paratrooper, Rick didn't need to use war speak. His final words to his wife were "Stop crying, I have to get these people to safety."

Teach your management a lesson by taking all business speech literally. Make your marketing strategy guerrilla by sabotaging your competition with a High T explosive device.

67. Regional Director Of Nothing

In your dingy little office in an outer suburb of a minor city, your old, decrepit manager decides to take an early retirement. You don't apply for the vacant role because managing a team of six seems like too much responsibility. You just don't want that kind of stress at the tender age of 30.

In 1403, a 16-year-old Henry (later, King Henry V) fearlessly led an army of 14,000 to crush a 10,000-strong rebel force in Wales. Ridiculously, you are scared to organise a small team meeting.

March into your boss's boss's office, sit in his chair, install yourself as CEO and start interviewing people to take the manager role.

68. Farm To Bin

Feeling a little peckish after a long day of clock-watching, you embark on a 'hunt' through your fridge. Bingo! You find a pack of mini cheese circles. However, after carefully reading the packaging, you see that they tragically went out of date yesterday. A tear slowly streaks down your face as you ceremonially bury them in the bin.

Until homo-erectus gained control of fire to cook meat around 1.5 million years ago, our ancestors devoured rotting boar carcasses straight off the bone. Any pathogens in the meat faced instant death in your stomach's Hydrochloric acid.

Commercially produced child snacks cannot harm you. Let them marinate in the bin juice and eat the whole pack, making your immune system so powerful that germs cower in fear.

69. It's A Jungle Out There

Despite your phone screen time exceeding 6 hours a day, you decide that the best way to find a girlfriend is to download yet another mobile app. You lay in bed, cock in hand, swiping right at every piece of cleavage you see. Through the paid upgrade and the sheer volume of swipes, you manage to get a date. However, due to the numerous filters, old pictures, and nuanced camera positions, she has royally fatfished you. This dinner is going to be even more expensive than anticipated.

There are roughly three times more men than women on dating apps. Women also swipe right six times less often than men. And although mathematically impossible, they rate 80% of men as below average looking.

Instead, take on a new side gig that allows you to meet lots of single women in person.

70. Screen Time Workout

After finishing one last half-rep at the gym, you rush to grab your phone, thinking a super important message might have come through. Inevitably, it has not. You naturally revert to doom-scrolling on Instagram, desperate for that next dopamine hit.

In life-or-death moments, adrenaline surges through our veins and boosts our heart rate, blood pressure, and alertness. The fact that you have the presence of mind to giggle at a video of a dog on a skateboard shows how pathetic your 'workout routine' has become.

Grab the heaviest dumbbell in the gym and feel the weight slowly crush your body. The fear of death will give you primal power, instantly making you the strongest person in the gym.

71. Sir Limp-A-Lot

It's been an exhausting day of answering questions and giving none in return at your brother's birthday BBQ, which he felt obliged to invite you to. One of his mates decides to host an after-party, and after circling the group, he hesitantly invites you, to which you respond, "I'll let you know". Everyone who previously accepted lets out a collective sigh of relief.

A recent study of my friend John found that 99% of the time, people who responded "I'll let you know" did not end up attending said event.

You should ALWAYS be in the know, and if you aren't, network until you are. Then let everyone know that you will not be attending their non-revenue-generating activity. Be a bro and say no.

72. Rich In Coupons, Poor In Life

You refuse to pay for parking, so you drive in circles, burning $10 of fuel until you find a free spot. You avoid toll roads, saving $5 in exchange for wasting the only finite resource – time. You buy the cheapest pair of shoes, only for them to disintegrate after a month.

Marcus Aurelius was the most successful Roman emperor, and part of his success was the value he placed on his time. "You could leave life right now. Let that determine what you do and say and think."

Live in the big picture game, let others fight for scraps. Rome wasn't built in a day but it was developed pretty damn quickly. Treat yourself like the ancient capital and get building.

73. Sleep Mode: Expert

As you often struggle to fall asleep, you developed a bedtime ritual of lavender spray on your silk pillowcase, rubbing one out to hentai porn, and then listening to soothing rain sounds. This is your complex attempt to wind down, despite having done nothing to wind up throughout the day.

During the catastrophic Apollo 13 lunar mission, three astronauts fought for survival after an on-board explosion crippled their spaceship. They finally paused after 25 hours to briefly rest in their cramped and freezing cabin.

Your body and mind should be so exhausted from mental and physical exertion that the opportunity to lie down in a safe and comfortable place is a miracle. Take a cardboard box to the street and learn to fall asleep to actual rain, rubbing one out to an actual woman who's walking by.

74. Orange Is The New White

After bragging to your friends about how tanned you are, you get caught out. A friend arrives at your house early, goes into your bathroom and sees you on all fours, spreading out your arse cheeks and spraying fake tan.

Tanning chemicals poison your body, but every time you spread your arse, it poisons your dignity. The sun sends 342 watts of solar energy to hit every square meter on Earth. You are not benefiting from any of this power.

Go outside and absorb that precious vitamin D. If your genetics don't allow it, then embrace your rawness and do something more productive with your day.

75. Soy Boy

As you get out of bed for another day of work that is yet to be automated, you know the only way you'll get through it is with your new favourite soy milk latte. Despite enjoying cow's milk since childhood, you've suddenly realised you have a lactose intolerance based on a fleeting comment from a tote-bag-wearing stranger.

Milk has sustained our species for ten thousand years, but you now think evolution has changed your stomach tolerance in the last three months.

Bring your cow to the coffee shop and milk that teat of wholesome goodness straight into your mug.

76. Stop In The Name Of MJ

You're strolling with your girlfriend when suddenly a maniac sprints by and snatches her dangling handbag. She looks over to you in horror as the criminal gains distance. You kiss her on the forehead and get ready for takeoff. In perfect cadence, you hit the ground. Heel, toe, heel, toe, heel, toe, wagging your hips as you go. She looks at you in disgust, "He's getting away, what are you doing?!". You reply, "Are you kidding? I'm not going to crease my Jordans".

Michael Jordan was able to dunk from the free-throw line in the same shoes, and you won't extend your toes in them because you want to preserve your $200 investment.

In the name of justice and protecting your woman, crease the hell out of the shoes and hunt that delinquent down. Let the crease communicate your abundance of wealth and utilitarian nature.

77. Struck Out

You finally managed to secure a date through an app and spent the last week planning the most exciting thing you could think of - 10-pin bowling and nachos. Assuming the only way you'll get a peck on the cheek is to reach a score of 100, you ask the receptionist to put up the side barriers. With a smug look on your face, you see your ball bounce from side to side before knocking down a few side pins. You confidently stride back, expecting your date to gaze at you with admiration.

The magnificent Taj Mahal was built as a shrine to the Emperor's wife, who died giving birth to their 14th child. It took 20,000 workers over 20 years to build. You may not be able to impress like an Emperor, but not being able to roll a ball in a straight line isn't a good start.

Hurl the ball as hard as possible. You might not finish 1st, but your brute strength and lack of care for social norms will get you straight to 3rd base.

78. King Of The Rats

As soon as you signed up for a long-term luxury car lease, your world collapsed when you got laid off by your manager. No job means no expensive dinners, no holidays, and perhaps not even a Friday night lapdance. Depression hits, and you can't see how life is worth living anymore.

Most humans' 'career' throughout history was subsistence farming - surviving solely off what they grew. A random drought would kill off entire villages through the torturous death of famine.

So, before you spiral into existential despair, thank your manager for giving you the gift of anti-consumerism. When you return to work, become so frugal you can make a single square of toilet paper last a week of shits. Then, once you've stacked enough cash, you can leave the rat race for the T-race.

79. Suck It Up

Whilst in a bar, 1st world problems are at large. Tired of lifting your cosmo all the way to your mouth, you ask the bartender for a straw. You suck the drink dry like a hungry anteater and make a loud gurgling sound as the final drops enter your mouth.

In the Norse mythological contest between the Giants and the Gods, Thor attempted to drain the ocean with three powerful gulps from his gigantic drinking horn. The only straw you should ever come into contact with should be the dried wheat variety after a long and plentiful harvest.

Berate any bartender who puts a straw in your drink. Then take it out and put it in the glass of the Lowest-T person you can find.

80. Voluntary Embarrassment

You boast to your friend about your new investment strategy, inspired by at least three TikTok reels. Each month, you now voluntarily allocate a slither of your miniature income to a retirement investment fund. You envision a luxurious golden retirement, all made possible by sacrificing your daily oat cappuccino budget.

Instead of contributing to a compulsory retirement fund, Grand Cardone built Cardone Capital, his own public retirement fund, which grew his net worth to over $600m.

The only information you need to absorb from "Barefoot Investor" is the need to be barefoot. You shouldn't be voluntarily contributing to anything but the sperm bank to ensure your High-T genes affect as many bloodlines as possible.

81. The Fast And The Feeble

You roll up to the lights in your eco-friendly shoebox on wheels, smugly admiring your low carbon emissions. You and your girl mates agree that real men only care about comfort, the environment, and saving money. "BZZZP.. .BZZZP...BZZZP low battery!" your car exclaims before coming to a halt in the middle of buttfuck nowhere.

In 1936, Bernd Rosemeyer strapped himself into a 500-horsepower death machine, attempting to break the land speed record on an open road. He hit 270 mph before a crosswind sent him—and the car—hurtling into oblivion. He died doing what modern cars have tried to erase - feeling alive behind the wheel.

Your vehicle should be an extension of your T. Get something that demands respect when you hit the throttle. If it doesn't make small children cover their ears and old men nod in approval, you've failed.

82. The Never Ending One Liner

At some soulless house party, you spend thirty minutes energetically droning on to your mates about how amazing you are. You aren't blinking, pausing for breath, or noticing that one by one, all of your mates have walked off. Suddenly, your nose starts bleeding and you realise you may have snorted too much cocaine again. However, to keep the comedown at bay, you leave the party and wait two hours to pay the drug dealer hundreds more dollars for another hit.

In Shakespeare's Hamlet, the famous "to be or not to be" soliloquy explores moral questions - whether death should be used as an escape, how fear of the unknown can paralyse action, and whether having a conscience makes us cowards. You, however, managed to speak for three times as long, covering topics a hundred times less interesting.

Become the cocaine dealer, and when people jump in your car to pick up, drive them miles into the countryside to take them on a wholesome walk.

83. The Wankathon

Whilst your friends are training for a marathon, you are pushing yourself in a very different way. Your friends will be cheered on by hundreds of bystanders, but the only applause for you is from the insidious pornography industry that has yet again stolen valuable time, friendships, and memories from a young male in the prime of his life.

In the first week of owning a smartphone, you saw more naked women than Henry VIII did in his entire life. This has led to 11% of men being self-reported addicted to porn.

Suss out which of your friends are the biggest victims of porn by the size of bags under their eyes and the look of defeat across their face. Hack into their phone and reroute their adult search traffic to Strava.

84. Tren Train

After 6 months of maxing out your newbie gains at the gym, you naturally start to develop body dysmorphia, fueled by your obsessive following of social media influencers and a belief that girls aren't interested in you because your rear delts don't pop enough. Of course, the only logical step is to jump on a steroid cycle recommended by a Broscience expert on Reddit and supplied by a 'chemist' who dropped out of high school.

When exposed to exogenous T, your body shuts down its natural hormone production. So at the end of your cycles, you'll feel like an 8-year-old girl, but with the tits of a 50-year-old woman.

Ditch the roid stack and simply stare at your naked body in the mirror until you develop an admiration for every muscle fibre in your body.

85. T Positive (T+)

Whilst on a cute evening stroll with your mum, you feel a sting as a mosquito bites you on the arm. "Ow! That's so itchy", you immediately whine, whilst vigorously scratching the area and gazing at your mum, desperate for emotional validation.

In 1912, Theodore Roosevelt was shot in the chest during a speech but continued anyway, proclaiming, "It takes more than that to kill a Bull Moose!"

Appreciate the mosquito's compliment that it chose to drink such High-T muscular blood, and watch as it now dominates the rest of its species.

86. Tyresome

As you are driving, you feel the front left tyre pop. You get out and wonder if you can change it yourself. It can't be that hard can it? You watched your grandma do it once and she had alzheimers and two fake knees.

Your dad might not have taught you how to change a tyre, but he also didn't teach you how to finger your girlfriend. You learned how to do that, though (presumably).

If you need some practice, break into your neighbour's garage and change all of their tyres, making you the village hero.

87. Undressing Your Pride

Tragedy strikes as you lose your best mate to marriage. But there's one last opportunity to go out with a bang - the bachelor party. What better way to enter a wholesome monogamous life than by going to a strip club? A place to be blue-balled by dozens of women that entertain your mediocre game, for $50 a song. You stumble home with inferior social skills and a raging boner, deciding to rub one out to stripper porn just to fall asleep.

Drake fell in love with stripper Maliah Michel and begged her to stop stripping. Despite all his fame and money, she decided to continue dancing anyway. Her daddy issues overpowered his mummy issues.

Before the show starts, swap out the strippers for your mate's mothers, curing this societal stain with some good old PTSD.

88. GTA Life

Entering your local train station, you carefully read all the cautionary signs. "Always hold the handrail", "Floor may be slippery when wet", "Don't run down the stairs". The graphic images show you what peril awaits if you defy these strict rules.

In the 1940s, Nazi Party member Oskar Schindler broke the law by falsifying records and bribing officials. He risked his life and, in doing so, saved 1,200 Jews from concentration camps. If he had cared about following the rules as much as you, then he would have driven the Jews straight to Auschwitz, and the film would have been called Schindler's Lift.

Every time you see a warning, do the opposite. These micro-protests will inspire the NPCs around you to wake up from their zombie state.

89. Warren Bluffett

You heard crypto is popping off from all of your mates at work, so you invest your measly savings of $200, meaning you'll have to use a credit card later in the month. You beaver away writing blogs about your financial strategy and preach incessantly to anyone who will listen. When asked how Crypto works, you freeze and start mumbling something about decentralisation, ledgers, and blockchain.

In 1637, during the Dutch Tulip Mania, people sold their homes and life savings to buy flower bulbs. When the market crashed, those holding the bulbs were left broke, humiliated, and flowerless. Crypto may be the future, but you, of all people, aren't the person to know.

You're not building wealth, you're rehearsing for the TED Talk no one asked for. Buy land, salt, and livestock. If your investment strategy can't feed a family or build a fortress, it's not a strategy.

90. Hyper Brainflation

After struggling to sustain a rare conversation with a woman (platonic of course), you realise you need to start binge watching Love Island so you can chatter your way through who's coupling up with who this week. Months later, you've managed to befriend multiple women, none of whom want to couple with you. On top of that, you've managed to quadruple your estrogen, which was already astronomical.

In 500 BCE, Chinese Confucian teachings advised men to focus on self-improvement, maintain a strong moral character, and foster positive relationships, rather than being preoccupied with the private affairs of others.

Fly over the Love Island and commence a carpet bombing campaign, thereby increasing global IQ by 5%.

91. Social Kamikaze

After sulking about your recent breakup, your friend Jessica tries to remedy the situation by taking you to karaoke. You gleefully accept, imagining how fun it will be to let your emotional trauma out. Several mojitos in, you sing a duet together, "Oh well oh well oh well oh, UH, tell me more, tell me more, did she put up a fight?"

In the early 1600s, Miyamoto Musashi actually did put up a fight. He was the greatest Samurai in history, winning over 60 duels with his iconic two-sword fighting style.

Karaoke is derived from the Japanese words for empty (kara) and orchestra (oke). It should be renamed Kara-T. Re-honour the right ancient Japanese traditions and take Jessica for a weekend retreat of intense Samurai training.

92. Points Millionaire

You struggle to contain your excitement as you realise you've nearly done it. It's taken months of shopping at specific stores, buying the right items at the perfect time. Yes, you've finally accumulated the required reward points to get 20% off a flight to a place you don't like, at the wrong time of year.

Shopping loyalty programs return an average of 1%. However, you'll end up spending 20% more at these stores.

The only loyalty you should have is to your tribe. When asked if you have a loyalty card at checkout, tell the Clerk that you earn respect, not points.

93. Sustainable Stupidity

To your surprise and delight, you somehow have $100 left over from your measly monthly paycheck. After seeing a YouTube advert of some dude in a rented Lambo, you decide to invest in "Environmental, Social, and Governance" (ESG) stocks, which align with your prepubescent worldview.

Being financially illiterate, you naturally pay little attention to their dismal financial forecasts, but enjoy the pretty annual report with pictures of smiling underprivileged kids planting vegetables. Well done, you really are ESG - An Extremely Stupid Guy.

Invest in whatever returns the most, which, given the current state of society, is probably testosterone replacement therapy.

94. Half Price Dignity

It's Saturday morning, and as you muster the strength to get out of your crusty bed sheets, the realisation dawns on you that today is Bae shopping day. Yes, the weekly tradition of trudging around a soulless shopping centre with the only girl you've managed to persuade to date you, mainly due to your promise to accompany her, and pay for her weekly retail therapy.

King Henry VIII spent his leisure days hunting wild animals with his peers, only returning to his tribe to feast on their bounty together. Tapping your credit card will hardly impress your girlfriend; however, it will drain your already non-existent financial resources.

Cut your bank card in half, collect some forest wood, and make the furniture yourself. This show of dedication will make you a King in her eyes, and avoid any conversation about the upcoming Autumn sales.

95. Selfie Sabotage

Your incessant need for validation prompts you to check your Instagram every 2 minutes. You can no longer work, read, or even socialise without fidgeting with your phone. Your pathetic beach selfie only has one comment, and it's "Nice to sea you" from stepdad. Validation fail, better check again soon. The phone-based life has even made you fearful of real-life interactions, no matter how innocuous.

Cher Ami was a pigeon who completed 12 successful WW1 missions, flying handwritten notes across enemy lines to provide intelligence for the Allies. The pigeon had to facilitate communication while avoiding machine gun fire, yet still had fewer self-esteem problems than you.

Go back to the style of communication before text, before email, and even before letter writing. Go up to someone and talk.

96. Splitting Atoms

It's a miracle; You and your best e-friends have aligned your enthralling lives to meet for a couple of drinks, during happy hour of course. After rambling about simulation theory and the pyramids, it's time to get the bill. Anxiety sweeps the table as you all realise that no one has the bank balance to cover the entire $75 and the bus ride home. An argument erupts as you each present the percentages of wedges, Mountain Dew, and tofu balls consumed.

For centuries, the Sikh Golden Temple has provided free meals to 100,000 people every day, rich or poor, sustained entirely by donations and the dedication of volunteers. Strangers share more time, effort, and resources with people they have never met.

You should be splitting empires, not bills. Tear up the receipt and slap the dweebs with a simulated hand of God, then take their remaining coins and donate it to people who really need it.

97. Temperatures At Boiling Point

Your pregnant wife's water has just broken, and you're frantically gathering all the supplies to rush to the hospital. You usher her into the car, turn the engine on, and calmly stare at the dashboard. Your wife starts to panic and shouts at you to drive, but you're busy monitoring the oil temperature to ensure it reaches 88 °C to avoid over stressing the pistons.

NASA rockets instantly burn at 7,000 degrees before hurtling into space. Your 1.0L Toyota Yaris can drive down a suburban street on a mild autumn afternoon without warming up.

Go pedal to the metal as soon as the engine starts. This will ensure your wife won't leave you to protect the baby from your Low-T tendencies.

98. Too Much Time On Your Hands

Being overly strategic about your fashion is certainly Low-T, but what could possibly be lower? Collecting watches. Spending more than you can afford on a small piece of metal to give you information that can be observed from the sun. And better yet, you have convinced yourself that this is bigger than fashion; it's an investment.

It is said that Steve Jobs never wore a wristwatch as he didn't want to be bound by time. A watch collection is merely a last-ditch effort at portraying value that you cannot display in other realms.

Besides, there is no need to know the time. If it's light outside, dominate and conquer men. If it's dark, dominate and conquer women.

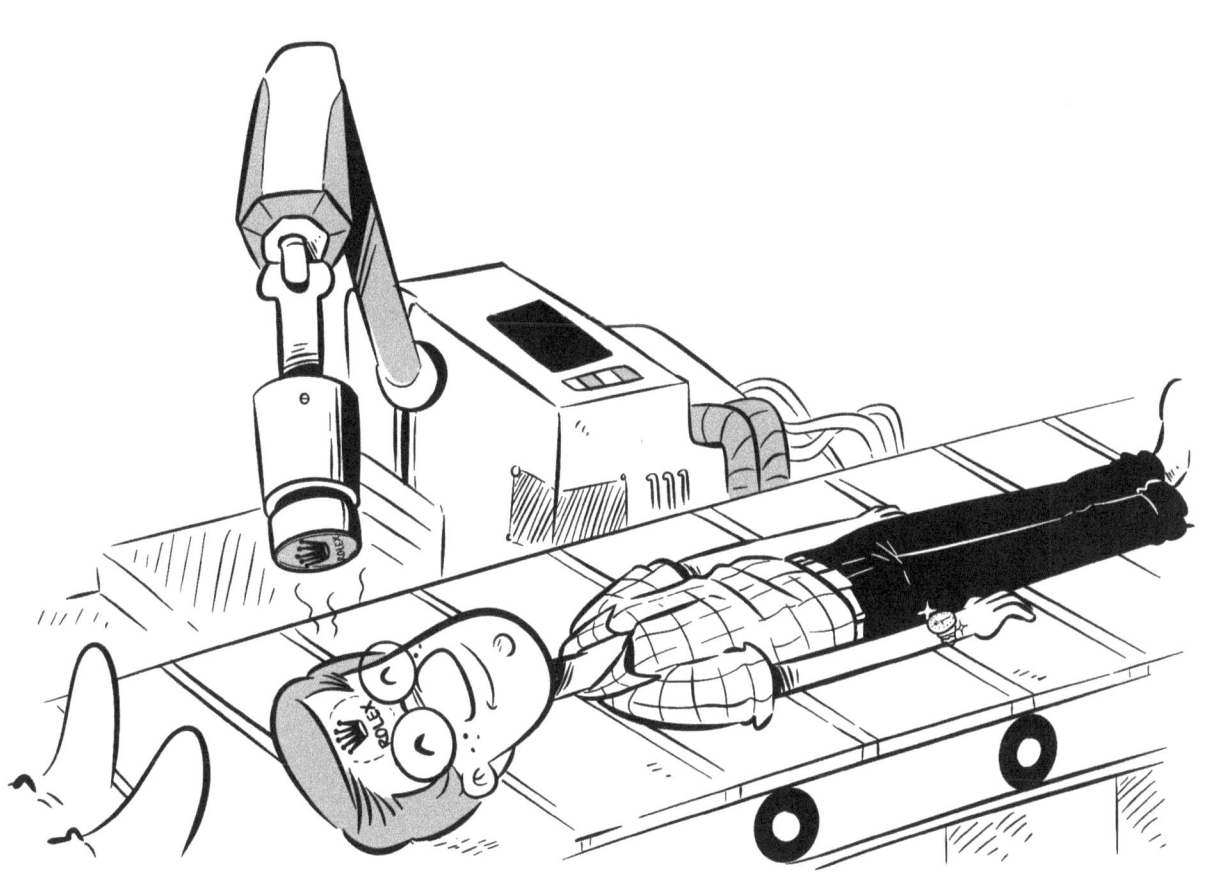

99. Bug Obliterator 9,000

Whilst watching TV at home, you hear a blood-curdling scream, one that can only mean that your sister has just seen a baby cockroach. As a seasoned veteran, you jump upwards, grab your bug-killing shotgun and head into enemy territory. Scanning the floor, you identify the target and eventually neutralise it with a nervous spray and pray approach. Your sister finds it sad that this has been your thrill for the day, as you sling the gun over your shoulder and head back to watching the Real Housewives.

During the battle of Okinawa, US medic Desmond Doss rescued 75 wounded soldiers from the battlefield in a single day, all whilst dodging artillery and refusing to carry a weapon.

Not everyone can be a real soldier, but at least act like one. Give the cockroach an honourable burial and reject any sense of achievement in killing a little insect.

100. The Selfless Gene

Without a girlfriend in sight, you still feel the need to comment to your friends that you don't want children. The reasons range from the personal to the political. You love the freedom of going to your all-inclusive beach holiday, and you talk about how selfishly having more children causes climate change.

Genghis Khan had 6 wives and 500 concubines, fathering ~3,000 offspring. Nowadays, over 16 million people are his descendants. To decide that your meaningless getaways and your sloppy understanding of the environment should result in you destroying a million-year-old bloodline is the most vacuous decision an individual can make.

Find the smartest woman you know and raise a tribe of baby Elon Musks that will solve climate change and save the world.

101. Your Own Truman Show

You notice friends on the verge of another existential crisis. Every morning, they ready their suit of armour against the world:

- Phone, so they don't see the beauty of the sunrise
- Headphones, so they don't hear the birds singing
- Sunglasses, so they don't see their neighbours
- Coffee, so they cheat the wake-up process
- Cigarette, so they don't breathe the fresh morning air

Despite Australia being one of the most prosperous countries in the world, 1 in 7 are now prescribed antidepressants.

But fear not, Dear Reader. You have already learnt 100 lessons to defeat modern crisis. Your remaining mission is help your tribe do the same by gifting them a copy of High-T 101.

www.ingramcontent.com/pod-product-compliance
Lightning Source LLC
Chambersburg PA
CBHW040116170426
42811CB00123B/1376